Wakefield I
& Informati

Andy Croft

Published in association with The Basic Skills Agency

Hodder & Stoughton

A MEMBER OF THE HODDER HEADLINE GROUP

Acknowledgements
Cover: Getty Images

Photos: p. 3 © Bill Ross/CORBIS; p. 7 © Paul A. Souders/CORBIS; p. 11 © Anne W. Krause/CORBIS; p. 15 © Galen Rowell/CORBIS; p. 18 © David Stoecklein/CORBIS; p. 23 © The Press Association Ltd 2001; p. 26 © Greg williams/Rex Features.

Every effort has been made to trace copyright holders of material reproduced in this book. Any rights not acknowledged will be acknowledged in subsequent printings if notice is given to the publisher.

Orders; please contact Bookpoint Ltd, 130 Milton Park, Abingdon, Oxon OX14 4SB. Telephone (44) 01235 827720, Fax: (44) 01235 400454. Lines are open from 9.00–6.00, Monday to Saturday, with a 24 hour message answering service. You can also order through our website www.hodderheadline.co.uk

British Library Cataloguing in Publication Data
A catalogue record for this title is available from the British Library

ISBN 0 340 87150 4

First published 2003
Impression number   10 9 8 7 6 5 4 3 2 1
Year   2009 2008 2007 2206 2005 2004 2003

Copyright © Andy Croft 2003

Typeset by SX Composing DTP, Rayleigh, Essex.
Printed in Great Britain for Hodder & Stoughton Educational, a division of Hodder Headline, 338 Euston Road, London NW1 3BH by The Bath Press Ltd, Bath.

Contents

		Page
1	Are You Tough Enough?	1
2	Air	5
3	Land	9
4	Water	13
5	Snow	17
6	Extreme Heroes	21
7	Really Xtreme	25

1   Are You Tough Enough?

Football, rugby,
boxing, cycling,
scuba diving,
rock-climbing,
Formula 1 –
all sports can be dangerous.

You have to be tough to do most sports.
If you don't train properly
you can get hurt.
Even river-fishing can be dangerous.
Every year more people die while fishing
than bullfighting!

But some people think
ordinary sports are not tough enough.
They like taking risks.
They like danger.
They like *extreme* sports.

You don't usually see extreme sports on TV.
You don't usually read about extreme sports
in the newspapers.
Some of them are against the law.
Most of them are very dangerous.
But you can't stop extreme sports.
There is even an extreme sport Olympic Games.
It takes place every year.
It is called the X Games.

A hang glider above the clouds.

Extreme sports are for extreme people.
You must be very tough.
You must be very brave.
And you must be a little bit crazy.

Extreme people look for adventure
in the air, on land, in water and on snow.

2 Air

Skydivers
jump out of a plane.
They don't pull their parachute for 80 seconds.
They fall through the air at 130 miles an hour.
They fall so fast they can't breathe.
Sometimes they dive head-first
so they will go even faster.
Sometimes they do somersaults in mid-air.
Sometimes they jump in groups
and hold hands on the way down.
If you don't pull your parachute in time
you are in big trouble.
SPLAT!

Hang-gliders
hang from the wings of a small glider.
They fly 10,000 feet up in the air
at up to 45 miles an hour.
Taking off is easy.
You just run about on the top of a hill
Until the wind lifts you into the air.
Gliding is easy.

You just float on the wind.
The hard bit is coming down.
BUMP!

Kite surfers

tie big, power-kites
to a beach buggy.
The wind blows the kite
and the kite pulls the buggy along the beach.
It is very exciting.
A strong wind can pull you along
at 20 miles an hour.
But the wind can also pull you
in the wrong direction.
BUMP!

Kite jumpers

run up and down on the end of a big kite.
When the kite starts to go up in the air
they don't let go.
When the kite flies away,
they fly away too.
Going up is easy.
But kite jumpers
come down to earth with a bump!
OUCH!

Bungee jumping.

BASE jumpers

jump off bridges and buildings
with a small parachute.
BASE jumpers have jumped off
the Eiffel Tower in Paris,
and the Empire State Building in New York.
BASE jumping is very, very dangerous.
It is also against the law.
BASE jumpers are killed every year.
Sometimes the jumper hits the ground
before the parachute opens.
CRUNCH!

Bungee jumpers

jump off bridges and cranes.
They are tied to a long piece of elastic
so they bounce back
just before they hit the ground.
Some people bungee jump over water.
If the bungee is too long you get very wet!
SPLASH!

3 Land

Adventure racers
race in extreme weather
through mountains and rivers,
forests and snow,
icebergs and deserts.

The *Canadian Death Race*
takes place every year.
Teams have to race 125 kilometres
over three mountains.
Then they have to cross
a big river at Hell's Gate Canyon.
It takes five days.
But they have to do it three times!
First they run the race in summer.
Then they race by bike in the autumn.
Then they race on snow-shoes in the winter.
They have to watch out for wild bears and wolves.
Crazy.

In the *Arctic Team Challenge*
each team has to walk, trek,
climb, canoe
and mountain bike across Greenland.
It takes five days.
It is very, very cold.
Each team has to carry their own food,
water and safety equipment.
They have to watch out for polar bears.
If they are not careful
they might be eaten!
Crazy.

desert runner.

Desert runners
like running for miles and miles
and miles and miles
and miles and miles.
They like running in the hottest weather.
They like running where it is dangerous.
They like running where it is lonely.
They even run across the Sahara Desert.
They don't mind blisters.
They don't mind sore feet.
They don't mind pain.
Crazy.

4 Water

Shark divers
swim underwater looking for sharks.
Sometimes they swim among little fish
when they are being attacked by sharks.

White water rafters
ride down mountain rivers,
over rapids and waterfalls.
They try to paddle
as they bounce between the rocks.
They also try not to fall out of the boat.

Cave divers

swim underwater and underground.
It is dark, cold and very dangerous.
You might get lost.
You might run out of air.
You might get stuck.
You might never get out.

Free divers

swim underwater as deep as they can
without any oxygen.
They take a big breath and then dive.
It is very dangerous.
If you swim too far
you will run out of breath
before you get back to the surface.
This means you will black out and drown.

White Water Rafters.

River swimmers
swim down the longest rivers in the world.
They swim all day and night.
The water is very cold.
They have to watch out for currents and whirlpools.
They have to watch out for ships and pollution.

5 Snow

Speed skiers
ski downhill as fast as possible.
They wear special suits to make them go even faster.
They can ski at 160 miles an hour.
It is very exciting.
It is very thrilling.
But one bump and you are dead.

A daredevil skier.

Extreme skiers
don't ski down hills,
they ski down mountains.
Like Mount Everest!
They ski near avalanches.
They ski through snow storms.
They ski near cliffs.
They ski through trees.
They don't care,
as long as it's dangerous.

Up-skiers
like skiing *up* mountains!
They tie themselves to a power kite
and let the wind pull them up.
When they reach the top
they ski back down.
Up-skiing is also called
'wind mountaineering'.

Snowboarders
are like skateboarders in the snow.
Their boards don't have wheels.
They just slide down the snow.
They go very fast,
up to 60 miles an hour.
You can't see where you are going.
You can't stop.
And you can't get off.
Snowboard racers race each other
down mountains.
The winner is the first one
to reach the bottom
in one piece.

6 Extreme Heroes

Ellen MacArthur
sailed round the world
on her own.
For a hundred days.
The waves were huge.
It was very cold and lonely,
especially near the south Pole.
A huge wave knocked her boat upside down.
Ellen had to jump in the water to get it upright.
She had no help.
It was freezing.
It took two days.
But she did it.

Martin Strel
is the world record river swimmer.
He once swam 3,000 kilometres
down the River Danube.
He swam 70 kilometres a day.
It took him 58 days.
It was the longest swim in history.
He once swam 500 kilometres in 84 hours
without stopping.
He is now planning to swim
4,000 kilometers down the River Mississippi!

Martin Strel swimming the river Donan.

Felix Baumgartner
is the world's most famous BASE jumper.
He holds the world record
for BASE jumping off the highest building,
and the lowest building.
One day he wants to hang glide
all the way from England to France!

Davo Karnicor
is the first person to ski down Mount Everest.
It took him 5 hours.

Tanya Streeter
is the world record free diver.
She once dived over 500 feet.
She was swimming underwater
for 3 minutes 26 seconds.
She once held her breath underwater for 6 minutes!

7 Really Xtreme

Have you had enough yet?
Or are you looking
for something really extreme?

Remember, you have to be extremely tough.
You have to be extremely brave.
And you have to be extremely crazy.

What about butt-boarding?
All you have to do is lie on a skateboard
and race down a road between the cars.
Butt-boarders go up to 80 miles an hour.

A bit too close for comfort?

You could try bull-riding or bullfighting.

Or climbing up the outside of buildings
using just your fingers.

You could try walking barefoot through fire.

Or sitting in a metal cage underwater
while sharks try to eat you.

You could try walking to the North Pole.

Or playing the piano
while you ski down a mountain!

How about camel races?
Or octopus-throwing?

If you are feeling really brave
you could try nude skiing or nude snowboarding.
You could try nude bungee jumping.
There is even a nude Olympics!

Some people will always take risks.
Some people will always look for danger.
Some people will always be extreme.

How extreme are you?